Show You Can Do

Heera Kang

Illustrated by Laura Gibbons Nikiel

Harcourt Achieve

Rigby • Saxon • Steck-Vaughn

www.HarcourtAchieve.com
1.800.531.5015

Level S

InStep Readers: *Show What You Can Do*

Dedicated to sweet Josephine, Colin, and Kira. All my love.

Text by Heera Kang
Illustrated by Laura Gibbons Nikiel

ISBN 1-4189-1069-4

Printed in China

1 2 3 4 5 6 7 8 9 10 285 09 08 07 06 05

Contents

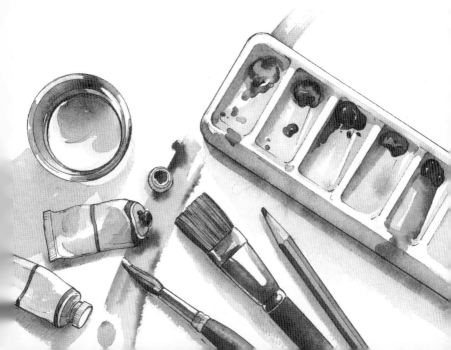

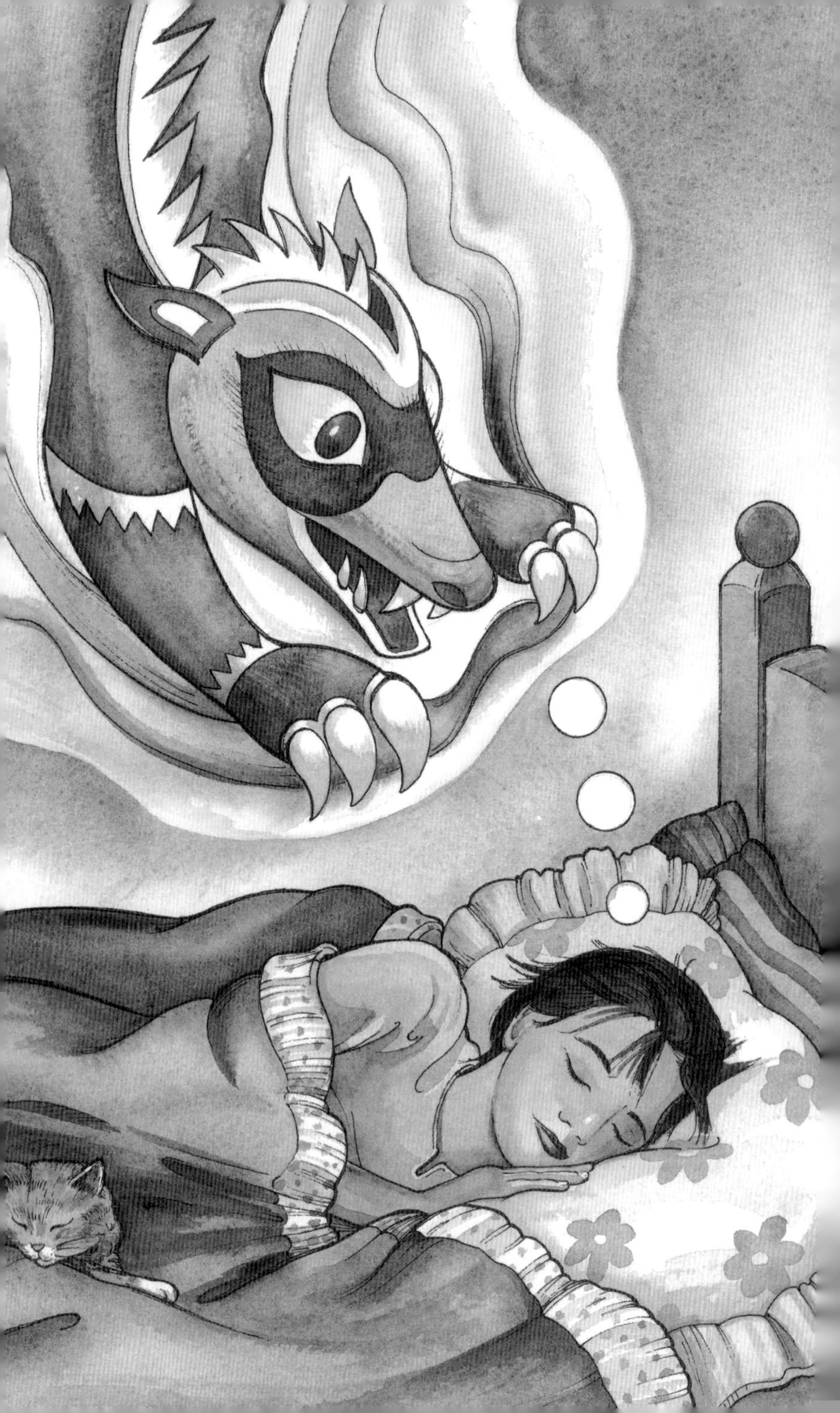

Chapter 1
A Bad Morning

The ugly, hairy creature crept slowly toward her, its yellow eyes burning brightly. It reached out its claw toward her face, moving closer and closer.

Miah Lee let out a muffled cry as she woke from the familiar dream. Her heart was beating wildly as she looked around for the creature. "I must have been dreaming. When will I stop having that nightmare?" she thought, lying back on her pillow.

The morning light peeked around the bedroom curtains. She was starting to feel better until she remembered that it was registration day for Camp Cassidy, a summer science camp. Miah shut her eyes again–she would rather face the creature in her dreams than think about Camp Cassidy.

There were only three months left until the end of seventh grade. Miah's parents had insisted that she sign up for Camp Cassidy because students who attended the science camp would be able to take advanced science in the eighth grade. Miah hated the idea of spending two whole months at a camp to learn about science.

Just then she heard someone opening her door, so she pretended to be asleep. Miah's older sister, Mijung, walked into the room and stood next to the bed.

"I can see your eyeballs moving behind your eyelids," said Mijung, "so I know that you're pretending to sleep."

"I have to register for Camp Cassidy today," said Miah in a depressed voice.

"Don't you remember how much fun I had when I went?" asked Mijung. "You get to meet new people, and there are all kinds of different activities."

Miah continued to look miserable even though Mijung said, "You'll have fun at camp. Now come downstairs for breakfast."

Miah watched her sister leave the room, and she thought about how much easier it would be if she were more like Mijung and enjoyed science. Their parents wanted both girls to do well in school, especially in science.

Miah thought about the parent night at school a few months before and remembered when her parents met her biology teacher.

"Miah earns good grades, but she just doesn't show interest in class," her teacher had told her parents. "She often looks like she isn't paying attention."

Miah had expected to be in trouble afterwards, but it seemed as if her parents had only heard the part about her good grades.

Miah crawled out of bed, picked up her sketchbook from the floor, and looked through the pictures she had been working on for the past few months. How could she make her parents understand that she wanted to study art, not science?

She wondered why she had to be so different from the rest of her family.

Chapter 2
Miah's Family

When Miah entered the kitchen, her mom was at the table, peeling fruit for everyone.

"Did you do your homework?" her mom asked. Miah's mom asked her that same question every morning.

"Yes," said Miah, holding out her math assignment for her mom to see. "That looks good, but next time, write your numbers more neatly," her mom said.

Miah's mother always looked at her math assignments closely because she was an accountant, and she was very good at math.

Miah's dad sat at the table, reading the newspaper and eating steaming noodle soup. For a second, the thought of hot, steaming soup distracted Miah from thinking about Camp Cassidy.

Mijung had finished her breakfast and was about to leave for school.

"Don't forget to take the registration form to school for Camp Cassidy," Mijung reminded her sister before walking out the door.

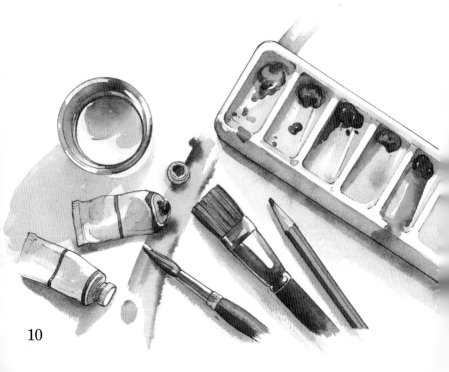

Miah's dad looked up from his bowl of soup and asked enthusiastically, "Do you have everything you need to register for camp?"

Her dad was a chemical engineer, and Miah couldn't help smiling as she imagined her dad as a seventh-grader going to the science camp. "He would have had a great time," she thought with a sigh.

Miah stopped eating her soup because she felt a nervous feeling in her stomach. "This would be the perfect time to tell them that I don't want to go to Camp Cassidy," she thought.

11

Miah really wanted to apply for the summer program at Juniper High School for the Arts. Students who went to the summer arts program had a better chance of being accepted into Juniper High School, and it was Miah's dream to go to there.

Miah opened her mouth to say something, but nothing came out.

She was always afraid to talk to her parents about her interest in art.

Once she received a low grade on a science assignment because she hadn't understood the instructions. That same week, she had also been working on a drawing. Miah's parents thought that she had spent too much time drawing and not enough time working on the science assignment. Since then, her parents always looked concerned any time they saw her drawing.

"You should be reading the next chapter for your science class instead of wasting time drawing pictures," her dad would say. Miah never drew in front of her parents anymore because she knew how it made them feel.

"No," she thought, "they'll never let me go to the summer arts program."

Miah sat in the kitchen staring sadly at her food. For once, her favorite soup wasn't making her feel better, so she pushed the bowl away and got up from the kitchen table.

"Miah, eat more!" her mom said. "Don't you want more soup?"

Just then, there was a knock at the door.

"Ah, Juliet, come in and have some soup!" Miah heard her mom say as she opened the door. Miah's good friend Juliet sat down at the table while Mrs. Lee placed a bowl of soup in front of her.

"Thanks, Mrs. Lee," said Juliet. She had just started to eat the soup when she noticed Miah giving her a look that said *Let's go.*

"Oh, uh, I forgot that we have to get to school a little early today. Thanks again for the soup, Mrs. Lee," said Juliet.

Chapter 3

The Creature Under the Porch

As the two girls walked out the back door and around to the street, Juliet saw Miah glance at the dark area under the front porch.

"Do you still think there's something under there?" asked Juliet. "You're getting too old to be scared of monsters."

"You're right," said Miah, "but you've never seen those creepy, yellow eyes!"

Miah first saw the creature under the porch a few years ago. She had been walking home one evening and had stopped suddenly in front of her house. She was sure she had seen something moving under the porch, and then she saw the eyes—the big, yellow eyes.

Miah couldn't move, and she was too embarrassed to call for help, so she decided to run down the street to her friend Juan's house. She had known Juan for a long time, and she knew he wouldn't tease her about it.

But when she returned to the porch with Juan, the eyes had disappeared. Juan told her that it was probably just a raccoon, but Miah had imagined a much larger, more frightening creature.

Now, whenever Miah went into her house through the front door, she would begin with a running start and leap up onto the porch as fast as she could.

Chapter 4
Juliet's Problem

At the end of the street, Miah and Juliet heard someone calling them. Juliet turned around to see Juan running toward them and yelling, "Hey, wait for me!"

"You're always making us late!" shouted Juliet. The three friends all lived in the same neighborhood and had known each other since third grade.

When they arrived at school, Miah went to her history class while Juliet and Juan walked to music class together.

Juliet avoided talking about Juniper's summer arts program in front of Miah, so as soon as Miah was far enough away, Juliet brought up the subject with Juan. "What am I going to do, Juan?" she cried. "I still haven't thought of what to send to Juniper for the summer arts program application!"

To apply for the summer arts program, students had to send in several pieces of artwork or a video of a performance.

Juliet had been playing piano for many years. She had plenty of videos of piano performances from her past recitals that she could send in with the application.

But Juliet knew that many of the other piano players applying for the program were very talented. "I don't want to send in an old video," said Juliet. "I know that I'm a better piano player now, and I wish I had a new video of a really special performance."

"Why don't you ask my mom for help?" asked Juan. Juan's mother, Mrs. Estrella, was the music teacher at Verde Middle School, and she was also Juliet's favorite teacher.

"Your mom has already helped me pick out some of my old videos," said Juliet, "but I want to send in something new!"

"Has Miah talked to her parents about the application yet?" asked Juan.

"No, and don't say anything to her about it because I've tried a hundred times," warned Juliet. "She doesn't want to talk about it because it just makes her sad."

Later that day, after music class, Mrs. Estrella asked Juliet, "Have you sent in your application for Juniper yet?"

"No, I haven't," replied Juliet, "but it's all I've been thinking about."

"Did you like any of the videos we picked out together?" asked Mrs. Estrella.

"They're fine, Mrs. Estrella, and thanks for helping me," said Juliet. "But I really want to send in something special for the application—something that stands out."

"I think it's wonderful that you're serious about this arts program, Juliet," said Mrs. Estrella, "but don't wait too long to decide."

Juliet knew she had to think of something very soon.

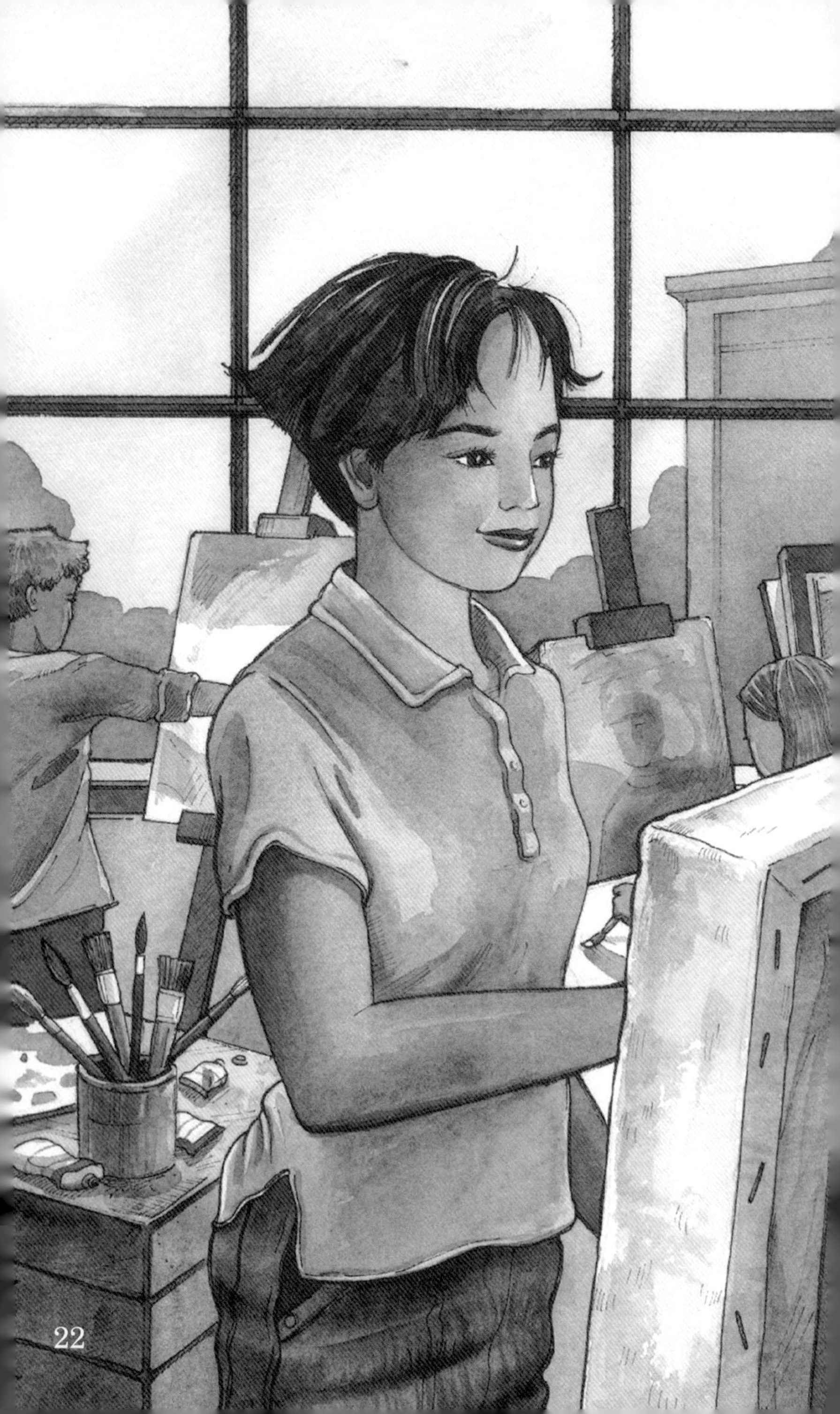

Chapter 5
Mr. Seiden's Advice

Miah felt upset during history class, and she felt even worse when she turned in her registration form for Camp Cassidy.

It wasn't until she went to Mr. Seiden's art class that she started to feel better. Miah forgot all about Camp Cassidy during art class, and she didn't even notice when the bell rang.

"Miah, " she heard Mr. Seiden say, "have you tried talking to your parents again about the summer arts program?"

Earlier that year, she had tried to ask her parents if she could apply for the program.

"You want to draw all summer long?" her mom had asked, looking at Miah in surprise.

"But you are so smart in science class," her dad had said. "If you don't go to Camp Cassidy, you won't be able to take the same classes that Mijung is taking in high school.

Miah shook her head and looked at Mr. Seiden. "I haven't tried to talk to them again," she replied.

Mr. Seiden looked at Miah silently for a moment, remembering how he had spoken with Miah's parents at the parents night. Though he had tried to tell her parents how talented Miah was, they had simply smiled and said "Thank you." "Miah, your parents were very polite, but they told me that they didn't think art was a serious subject to study."

"It's serious to me," Miah muttered sadly.

"Miah, I know how much art means to you, and you're very talented," said Mr. Seiden, "so maybe you could try talking to your parents again this weekend. You still have time to choose some of your drawings to send in with the application."

Miah played with her jacket zipper while Mr. Seiden spoke. She had heard this advice before, and though she liked Mr. Seiden very much, she knew there was no way to change the way her parents thought.

"Thanks, Mr. Seiden. I'll think about it," said Miah, and she left to go to her next class.

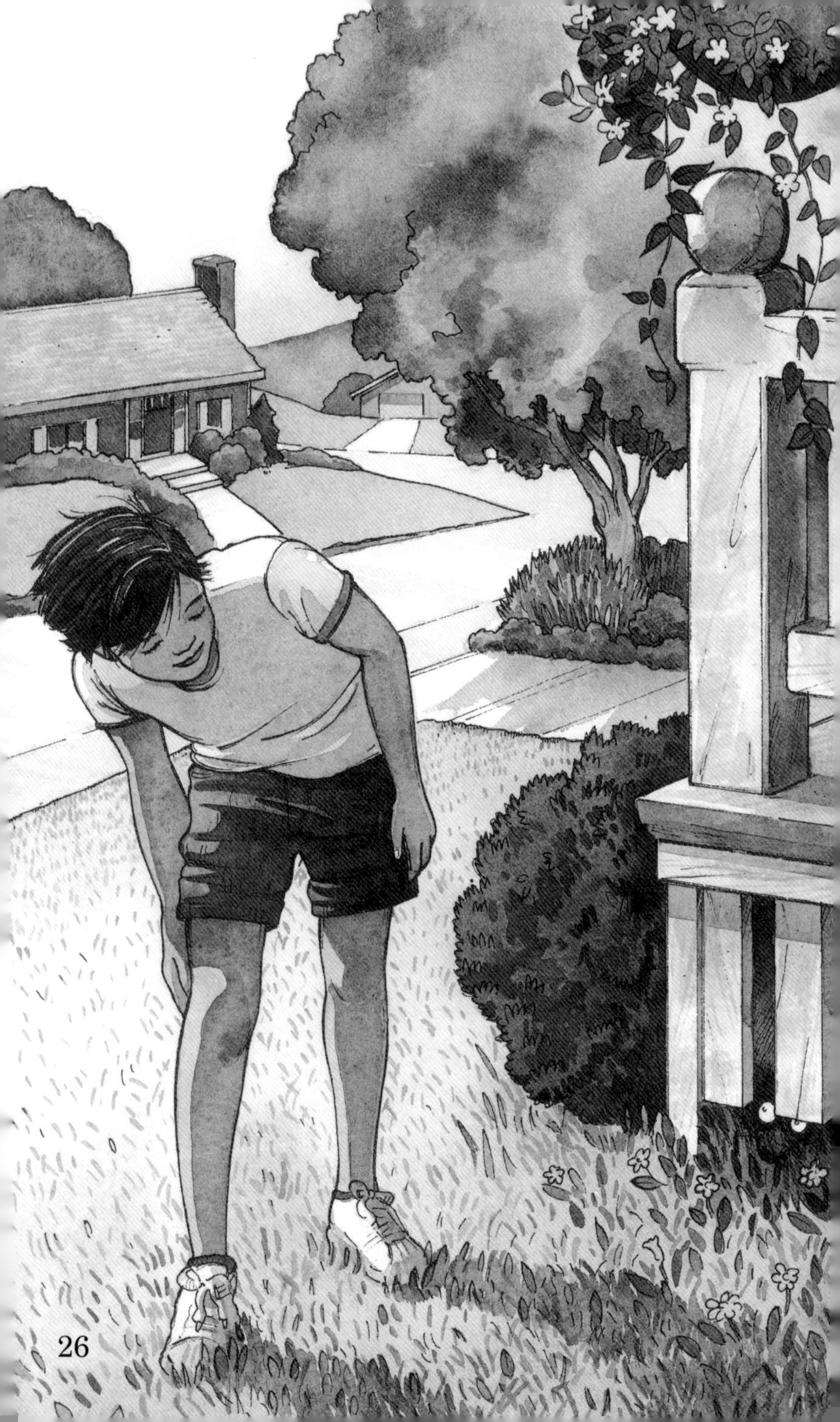

Chapter 6
Mrs. Lee's Secret

On Wednesdays Miah usually visited her aunt who lived nearby. As Miah jogged down the front porch steps on the way to see her aunt, she tried not look under the porch. She couldn't help it, though, and she quickly turned her head away when she saw the yellow eyes. Was she imagining it, or was she seeing the creature a lot more often lately?

She hurried toward her aunt's house, angry with herself for looking under the porch at all.

At her aunt's house, Miah played jacks with her younger cousin, Soojin. Their grandmother had brought back the special jacks from her last trip to South Korea, and Miah and Soojin loved to throw the colorful little jacks and catch them on the backs of their hands.

Miah tried to have fun, but she couldn't stop thinking about Juniper. She was so distracted that when it was her turn to throw the jacks, she missed every single one. Feeling frustrated, she started to cry.

"Soojin, please watch your television show while I talk with Miah," said her aunt.

When Miah was too young to remember, her aunt had hurt her arm very badly in a car accident. After the accident, Miah's family visited her aunt every week to spend time with her. Miah was very close to her, but she hadn't told her favorite aunt about the summer arts program. She thought that her aunt might try to talk to her parents about it, and Miah didn't want to get into trouble.

But Miah was so upset now that she told her aunt everything about the summer arts program and how she wanted to attend Juniper High School.

"There's nothing I can do about it," Miah sobbed, "because my mom and dad don't want me to draw. They don't listen to me and they don't understand how important art is to me. I'm nothing like them!"

After a moment, her aunt opened the closet door and said, "I want to show you something, Miah."

Her aunt opened a big, old cardboard box, and Miah saw that the box was filled with records.

"These were your mother's records, and she gave them to me years ago," her aunt explained. "Have you ever noticed what a beautiful voice your mother has? Did you know that she wanted to be an opera singer?"

"But my mom is an accountant," Miah said, feeling stunned and very confused.

"She is now, but when she was your age, she collected as many opera records as she could," explained her aunt. "After your parents got married, she decided to do something else for work. Your father enjoyed listening to opera music, too, and his favorite song was *"O Mio Babbino Caro."* It was written by an Italian composer named Puccini," said her aunt, handing Miah a record.

Miah didn't know what to say as she ran her finger along the hard outside edge of the record.

"Your parents want you to be happy," explained her aunt, gently. "Can you see now that you are not so different from them? Do you think you could talk to them?" she asked.

Miah nodded excitedly as she kissed her aunt on the cheek and rushed out the door toward Juliet's house.

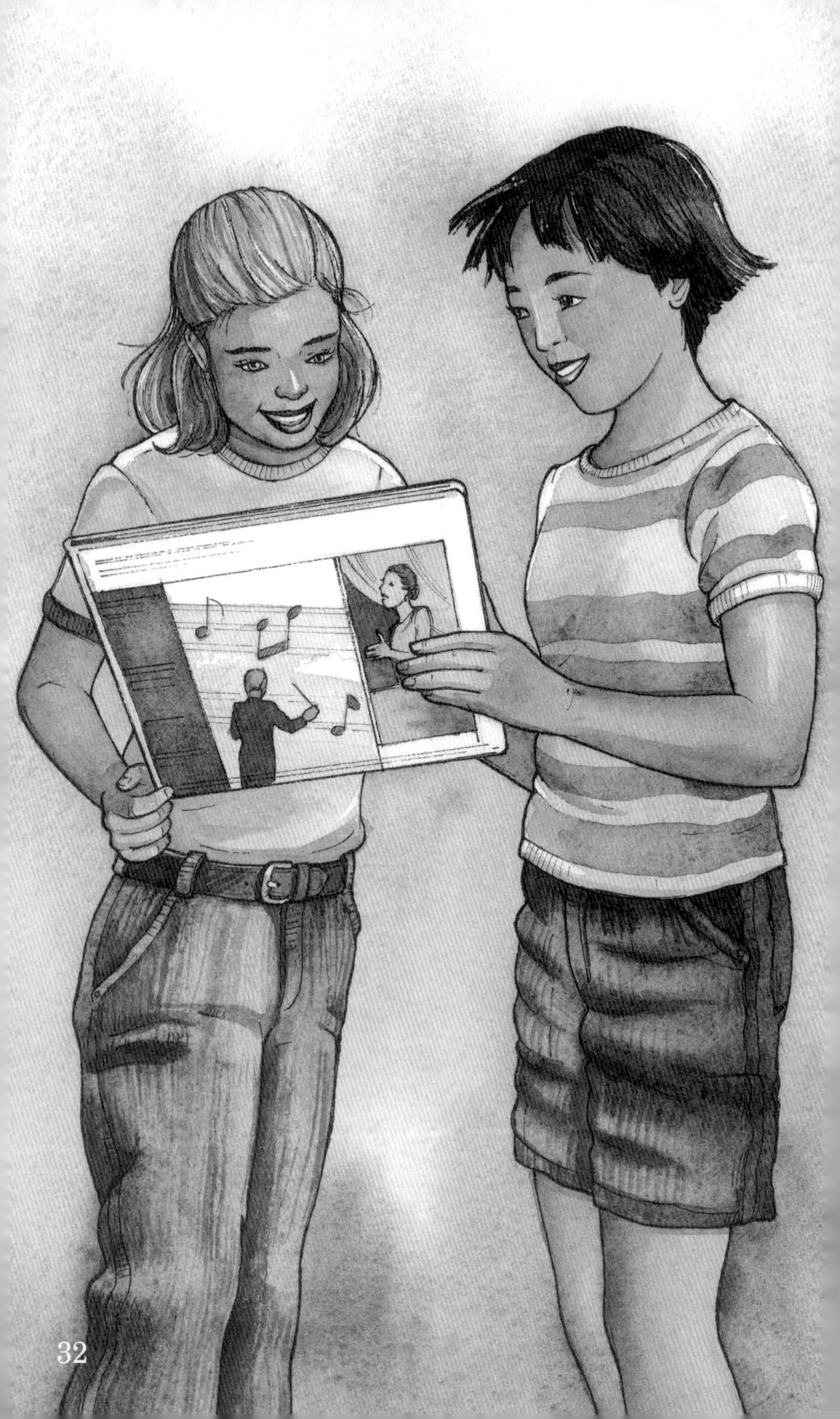

Chapter 7
Bad News

At Juliet's house, Miah couldn't tell the story fast enough. "So my mom wanted to be an opera singer!" cried Miah.

Miah showed Juliet the record of her parents' favorite opera song.

"I played that song at a recital once!" Juliet said. "It's so beautiful." Then she decided to tell Miah that she was applying to Juniper, but she had been struggling to choose a video to send with her application.

"Juliet, why didn't you tell me about this before?" Miah asked, her smile fading. "You don't have to feel bad about applying to Juniper," said Miah. "Maybe you could play this song for your application!"

"Let's go to Juan's house so you can tell him about your mom, and I'll ask Mrs. Estrella what she thinks about the song!"

Miah and Juliet arrived at Juan's house bubbling with excitement, but when Juan answered the door, he looked upset.

Miah and Juliet went in the house and saw Mrs. Estrella in the living room, sitting on the sofa with tears in her eyes.

"I have some bad news," said Mrs. Estrella. "This afternoon Principal Wheeler announced to the art and music teachers that there will be large budget cuts at our school next year. What this means is that Verde Middle School will not have the money to keep its art and music classes."

"What about all of us?" asked Juliet, looking confused. "And what will you and Mr. Seiden teach next year?"

"We'll have to look for jobs at other schools, Juliet," said Mrs. Estrella. "I've already made some phone calls, and there may be a job for me in Corona County."

Miah knew that Corona County was about two hours from where they lived, and she couldn't imagine school without Juan, Mrs. Estrella, and Mr. Seiden.

"Mrs. Estrella, do you think Principal Wheeler would let the music and art students organize a show?" asked Miah. "Maybe if we can show the school what we can do, they'll see that cutting those classes would hurt so many talented students, and they might decide to keep the classes."

"I'm not sure if there's anything that can be changed now, but I think it would be a wonderful idea for the students to have a chance to show their talents," said Mrs. Estrella. "I'll speak with Mr. Wheeler about it in the morning."

As they continued to talk about the show, Miah also told Juan and Mrs. Estrella about her mother's interest in singing opera music.

"Now I know that I can talk to my parents, especially my mom, and I can try to make her understand that I feel the same way about art as she did about singing," said Miah, sounding confident.

Juliet told Mrs. Estrella about the song that she wanted to play for her Juniper application video.

"I wanted to do something really special for my application, and now I know what to do!" said Juliet. "If we have a show, then I can perform the song." Juliet described an idea that would combine her music with Miah's artwork.

"We could videotape the performance at the show," added Juliet "and I can send in the video with my Juniper application! And after the show. . . ."

"After the show, I'll talk to my parents," said Miah.

Chapter 8

Preparing for the Show

Principal Wheeler approved the show, so Miah, Juliet, and Juan spent the next four weeks preparing for their performances. Finally, the day of the show arrived. After their last class ended, Juliet and Juan ran to the music room to borrow some supplies for the show later that night. There they found Miah sitting in the room.

"I can't believe that the show is tonight," said Miah softly as Juliet and Juan walked into the room. "Our lives could change a lot in the next month." The friends were feeling a mixture of emotions—they were excited about the show, but they were worried about whether their plan would work and if the school would keep the art and music classes. Also, Miah couldn't stop thinking about what she was going to say to her parents.

"Let's just try to have fun tonight," said Juliet, "because it might be the last time we get to do something like this together." Juliet wanted to make everyone feel better, but Miah couldn't help feeling nervous.

Miah still felt anxious as she arrived at her house after school. She started her usual leap up the porch steps, but this time she wasn't paying attention, and she lost her balance on the top step. Down she tumbled, hitting the ground face first. Her head felt like it was spinning, and she hurt all over.

There, on the ground, unable to move, she pictured her mother as a 13-year-old girl. She saw her secretly listening to opera records and singing her favorite song, *"O Mio Babbino Caro"* to herself in her room.

Miah had her eyes closed, so she didn't notice that there was something moving under the porch. She slowly opened her eyes and saw a big, hairy raccoon staring at her through the gap in the steps. Miah froze. She looked closely at its eyes, and she knew that she was looking right at the creature under the porch!

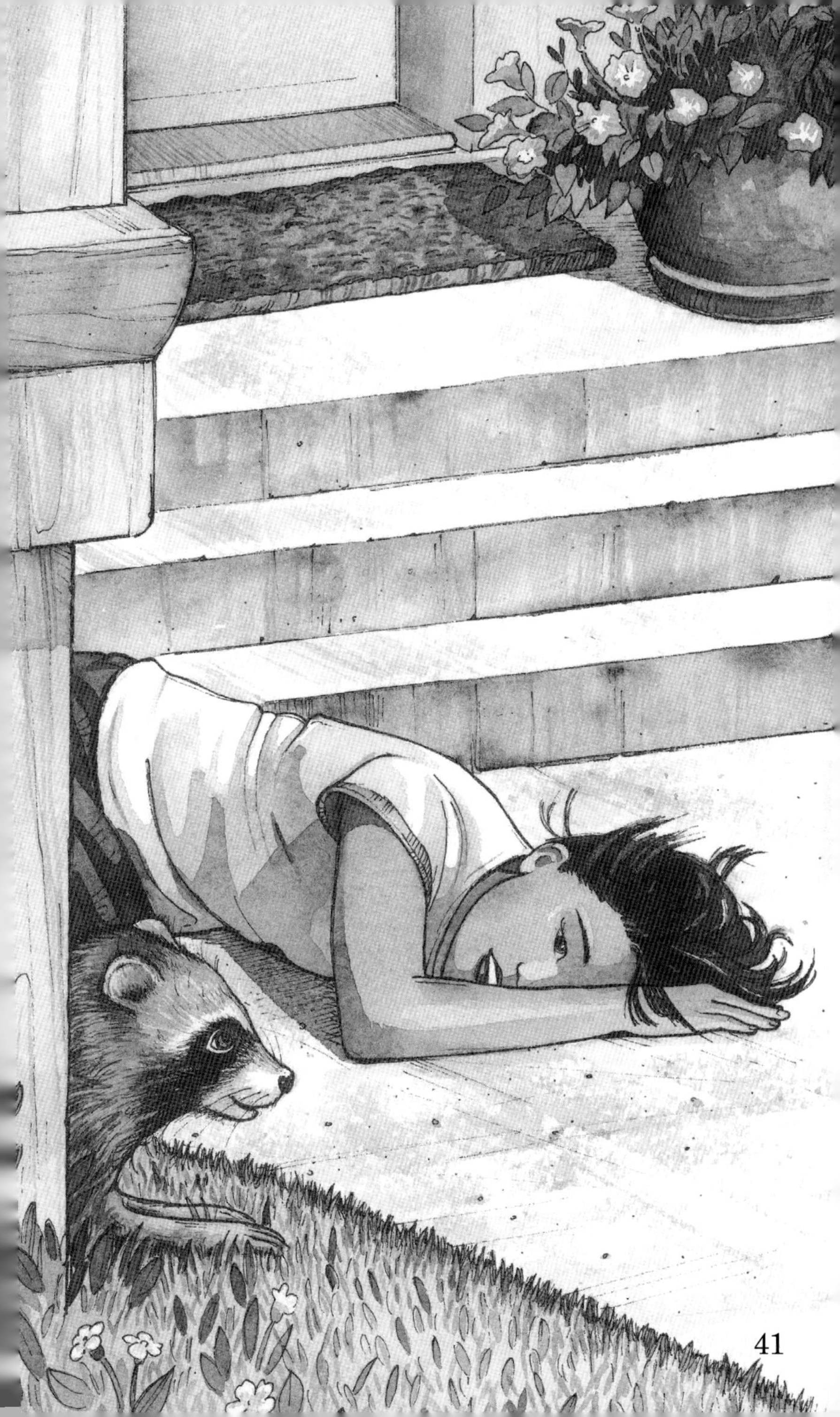

The raccoon stayed very still. At first, Miah considered grabbing the broom that was on the porch and scaring the raccoon away. However, when she started to move, she noticed that the animal's eyes were opened very wide, and that its whole body was shaking. The creature under the porch with the creepy yellow eyes wasn't going to hurt her—it was scared of her! She thought about the nightmares she had had about the creature and how she always felt scared going into her house. Suddenly she wasn't afraid anymore.

Miah slowly pulled herself up, keeping her eyes on the raccoon under the porch. She was surprised to see that the raccoon was staring at her, too, as if he were waiting for her to hurt him. "It's OK. I won't hurt you," Miah said, "if you don't hurt me." Miah was soon standing, the bruises and scrapes on her arms stinging a little.

Even though she ached, Miah slowly stood up and took a deep breath—she felt like she could do anything now. She wasn't anxious about talking to her parents anymore. "If I can face the creature under the porch, I can definitely face my parents!" she thought.

Chapter 9
Facing Fears

There was a hum of excitement in the air, and all of the students who were performing that night had nervous but happy looks on their faces. Miah met Juan and Juliet backstage at the school's auditorium.

"Miah, what happened to you?" cried Juliet when she saw Miah.

"I fell," Miah explained, showing her friends the bandage on her hand and the bruises and cuts on her arms and face. By the time Miah told them what had happened, it was time for the show to start.

The teachers gathered all the performers together for one last talk.

"We know each of you has worked extremely hard practicing for this show," said Mr. Seiden. "I want you to look around at everyone here and see what a talented group of students you are."

As all the students performed, Juliet, Juan, and Miah could see that the audience was impressed. The audience applauded after the art students presented all kinds of artwork: sculptures, paintings, and drawings. Music surrounded the audience as other students played flutes, guitars, and even trumpets and drums.

Then Mr. Seiden announced, "As you know, we have some very talented students at Verde Middle School, and they all planned their performances entirely on their own." The audience applauded before he continued, "Finally, I'd like to introduce our last musical performance by Juliet Luce with artwork by Miah Lee."

The lights dimmed, and soft music began playing as images of Miah's art flashed on a screen. The spotlight shined on Juliet as she played *"O Mio Babbino Caro"* on the piano. Miah used the projector to flash different drawings on the screen behind her. Each drawing matched the mood of the music. Mrs. Estrella stood at the back of the auditorium and videotaped the performance.

Miah looked out into the audience and could see her parents' eyes shining. The entire crowd was completely silent as they listened and watched.

At the end of the performance, the crowd stood up and applauded, and Miah saw her parents and sister clapping loudly.

"We haven't heard that song in a very long time," Miah's father said when Miah joined her family.

"I didn't know that your drawings were so musical," her mother added, and everyone laughed.

"Does this mean you'll reconsider letting me go to Juniper summer arts program instead of Camp Cassidy?" Miah asked hopefully.

"At Juniper you will improve as an artist," her father said, "and you will be happy."

"You have two daughters who are very talented–each in her own way," said Mr. Seiden as he approached Miah and her family.

"We are very lucky," agreed Mrs. Lee, looking at Miah.

On the other side of the auditorium, Juan and Mrs. Estrella waved for Juliet to join them, and Mrs. Estrella gave Juliet a big hug. "Your performances were so good that Principal Wheeler told me that he's going to talk to the school officials and try to keep the art and music classes next year!"

Juliet was extremely relieved, but before she could say anything, Miah had rushed over to them.

"My parents said that I can apply to the summer arts program! I don't have to go to Camp Cassidy!" cried Miah. "They really loved the song, Juliet, and they were really impressed by my drawings."

Everyone congratulated each other, and the auditorium became a noisy celebration after the show.

Juliet looked at the bandage on Miah's hand and the cuts and bruises on her face.

"Miah, you look like you've fought a battle tonight," said Juliet.

In a way, Miah felt like she *had* fought a battle—and won.